ANCIENT EGYPT

Written by Anita Ganeri

FRANKLIN WATTS

LONDON•SYDNEY

Franklin Watts
Published in paperback in Great Britain in 2019
by The Watts Publishing Group
Copyright © The Watts Publishing Group, 2017
All rights reserved.

Editor: Sarah Silver
Designer: Matt Lilly
Picture researcher: Diana Morris

ISBN 978 1 4451 5309 4

Ashwin Kharidehal Abhirama/Dreamstime: 19t. Ancient Art and Architecture/ Alamy: 26t. Jon Arnold/Alamy: 22b. Richard Ashworth/Robert Harding PL: 8t. RichardBakerEgypt/Alamy Stock Photo: 16. BasPhoto/Shutterstock: 22t. Boobsie/ Dreamstime: 15b. Christophel Fine Art/Getty Images: 13. Ivy Close Images/Alamy: 20br. De Agostini/Superstock: 25. Werner Forman Archive/HIP/Alamy: 26b. Paulo Gallo/Shutterstock: 24. Dieter Hawlan/Dreamstime: 10b. Hulton Archive/Getty Images: 28t. Ileana bt/Shutterstock: 7t. Interfoto/Superstock: 15t. Anton Ivanov/ Shutterstock: 4. Lenteja/Shutterstock: 12c. Amanda Lewis/Dreamstime: 18b, 19c. Look and Learn: 6. Alberto Loyo/Shutterstock: 21b. David Parsons/istockphoto: 9. Andrei Petrachkov/Dreamstime: 20br. prapass/Shutterstock: 11cr, 17, 23, 29t. Prisma Archivo/Alamy: 27b. Yulia Ryabokon/Dreamstime: 19b. Sibyl Sassoon/ Robert Harding PL/Superstock: 8b.Ignasi Such/ Dreamstime: 14b. swisshippo/ Dreamstime: 10t. Tepic/Dreamstime: 28b. Universal Images Group/Superstock: 12b, 15t. Paul Vinton/Shutterstock: 15br. Waj/Shutterstock: 21t. Wikimedia Commons: 5. Wisconsinart/Dreamstime: 3, 27t. WitR/Shutterstock: front cover. Vladimir Wrangel/Shutterstock: 11cl. Vladimir Zadvinskii/Dreamstime: 18c. Martin Zak/Dreamstime: 7b.

FSC
www.fsc.org
MIX
Paper from
responsible sources
FSC® C104740

Printed in China

Franklin Watts
An imprint of
Hachette Children's Group
Part of The Watts Publishing Group
Carmelite House
50 Victoria Embankment
London EC4Y 0DZ

An Hachette UK Company
www.hachette.co.uk

www.franklinwatts.co.uk

Contents

4   Who were the ancient Egyptians?

6   Ancient Egyptians at home

11   **WRITING HISTORY:** *A scribe's letter*

12   Pharaohs and wars

17   **WRITING HISTORY:** *Interview with a pharaoh*

18   Gods and beliefs

23   **WRITING HISTORY:** *Day in the life*

24   Death and the afterlife

29   **WRITING HISTORY:** *Newspaper report*

30   Glossary and Further Information

32   Index

Who were the ancient Egyptians?

The ancient Egyptians were the people who lived in Egypt more than 7,000 years ago. From a group of small villages, ancient Egypt grew into one of the greatest civilisations in the world.

In time, the villages formed two kingdoms – Upper and Lower Egypt. Then, in around 3100 BCE, King Menes united the country, and built his new capital at Memphis.

The River Nile flowing through Egypt today.

Ancient Egypt

Most of Egypt is covered in hot, dry desert where very little can grow. The ancient Egyptians called this 'the Red Land' and considered it a dangerous place. They lived on narrow strips of land along the River Nile. The river was vitally important to Egypt's survival and success. It provided fertile land, called 'the Black Land', for farming, water for irrigation and was Egypt's main transport route.

Ancient Egypt

Around 3100 BCE	King Menes unites Egypt
Around 2649–2150 BCE	The Old Kingdom
AROUND 2590 BCE	The Great Pyramid at Giza is built
Around 2040–1640 BCE	The Middle Kingdom
Around 1552–1069 BCE	The New Kingdom
Around 1347–1337 BCE	Reign of Tutankhamun
Around 1289–1224 BCE	Reign of Ramesses II
196 BCE	The Rosetta Stone is carved
51–30 BCE	Reign of Cleopatra VII
30 BCE	Egypt becomes part of the Roman Empire

ANCIENT WRITING

In the late 19th century, archaeologists discovered a large, flat piece of stone in Egypt. It was carved with pictures and writing, and dated from around 3000 BCE. On one side, the stone showed King Narmer wearing the white crown of Upper Egypt; on the other, the red crown of Lower Egypt. Many experts think that King Narmer and King Menes were the same person.

WRITING HISTORY

Much of what we know about history comes from written accounts and records that have been left behind. Throughout this book, you will find panels asking you to write your own versions of the history you have read. You will find the information you need in the book, but you can also look online and in other books. Use the tips provided, and don't be afraid to let your imagination run wild.

The stone is called the Narmer Palette, after King Narmer.

Ancient Egyptians at home

How you lived in ancient Egypt depended on whether you were rich or poor. Rich people lived in large spacious houses, and wore expensive jewellery and beautiful clothes. Poor people had much smaller houses, often with only one room for the whole family. They wore simpler jewellery and worked very hard on the land.

House design

A rich Egyptian's house could have as many as 30 rooms. At the front was a reception area where business was done. Behind that was a columned hall for entertaining guests, and at the back of the house were the family's private rooms. Inside, the house was decorated with fine wall paintings. Outside, there might be shady gardens, with a well-stocked fish pond. For poor Egyptians things were not so luxurious. Cooking was done outside the house, to reduce the risk of fire. On hot nights, people may have slept on the roof. The houses were simply decorated, with very little furniture.

Did you know?

Family life was very important to the ancient Egyptians. They considered children to be a blessing from the gods. Boys tended to follow their fathers' profession, and some boys from wealthy families went to school. Girls helped their mothers at home, though there are records of some becoming priestesses and doctors.

An artist's impression of a wealthy Egyptian's courtyard.

Egyptian fashion

The ancient Egyptians wore clothes made from linen, which was light and cool. For men, the basic dress was a simple kilt, made from a length of linen wrapped around the waist, and tied with a knot. Women wore long, tunic-style dresses. In winter, people wore shawls or cloaks. People often went barefoot or wore sandals made from papyrus reeds. Fashions changed very little throughout ancient Egyptian times.

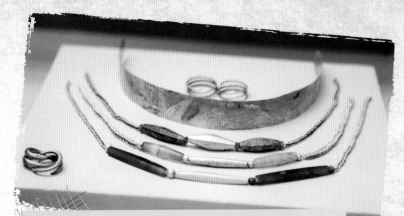

A selection of jewellery from ancient Egypt, on display at the British Museum in London.

Fabulous jewels

From archaeological evidence, it seems that everyone in ancient Egypt wore jewellery. Poor people wore simple pieces, made from pottery and cheap metals, such as copper. But rich people could afford beautiful earrings, bead collars and pendants. They were made from gold and silver, and inlaid with semi-precious stones.

This tomb painting shows ancient Egyptian men in simple kilts.

Write an advert

Try writing an advert for an on-line shop, selling ancient Egyptian clothes. State briefly what the item is, such as a kilt, giving a choice of colours and sizes, if applicable. Then talk about any special style features it might have.

Floods and farms

Most ancient Egyptians worked as farmers on large estates belonging to wealthy landowners. They gave part of the crop harvest they grew to the landowner as rent. Farming was made possible by the River Nile. Each year, the river flooded, depositing rich soil on the fields.

Did you know?

Bread was an important part of the ancient Egyptians' diet, but also one reason for their terrible teeth. Grain was ground between two stones to make flour. Because this was usually done outside, the flour often contained grains of sand and grit. This made the bread very tough to chew and quickly wore people's teeth down.

Well watered

The river also provided water for irrigation, essential in such a hot, dry country. Irrigation canals were dug from the river to the fields. To raise water from a lower to a higher level, farmers used a shaduf. This was a beam, with a weight on one end, and a bucket on the other. The farmer dipped the bucket in the river, let the weight lift it up, then poured the water into the canal.

A shaduf in use today.

The farming year

Inundation
(July to September)

While the river floods, work has to stop. Some farmers are called up to work on royal building projects, such as tombs or temples, or in the mines.

Summer
(June to July)

The ground is too hard to dig, so farmers spend time repairing the irrigation canals, ready for the next flood.

Growing season
(October to February)

The floodwaters go down, leaving a layer of rich, black soil behind. The farmers plough their fields and sow seeds.

Harvest
(March to May)

The taxmen come to assess how much grain has to be paid to the pharaoh. The crops can then be harvested.

Write a farmer's blog

Imagine that you are an Egyptian farmer, keeping a blog about your year. (A blog is a diary that you write online.) Write a post for each season, describing your work. Your blog will most likely be read by other farmers, so you can use friendly, informal language.

Special gauges called nilometers were used to check the river levels during the flood season.

Egyptian writing

The ancient Egyptians used an alphabet made up of pictures called hieroglyphs, which stood for objects and sounds. These were reserved for important inscriptions, such as those on temples, tombs and official records. For daily use, a simpler, quicker script was used.

These Egyptian hieroglyphs have been carved into stone.

Scribe school

Hieroglyphs were extremely complicated, and only professionally-trained writers, called scribes, could use them. Training began when a boy was around nine years old, and lasted for four or five years. Scribes wrote with ink and reed brushes. They practised writing on pieces of broken pottery. Once they were good enough, they were allowed to write on papyrus scrolls. Good scribes were highly valued, and could rise to important jobs in temples or in the government.

ROSETTA STONE

When the Romans conquered ancient Egypt, the use of hieroglyphs died out. For centuries afterwards, no one knew how to read them. Then, in 1799, a French soldier found a stone slab in Rosetta, Egypt. On it, the same text was written in three scripts – hieroglyphic, demotic and Greek.
By comparing the three, experts were able to decipher hieroglyphs.

The Rosetta Stone is on display in the British Museum in London.

Writing History: A Scribe's letter

Imagine that you are a trainee scribe who has just started at scribe school. Write a letter to a friend about your new life. The opening of the letter has already been written. Tell them about the sort of things you do, and how you feel about your training. Are you enjoying it? Are hieroglyphs very hard to learn? What are your hopes for the future?

Scribe School
Thebes
Egypt

Summer, 1375 BCE

Hi Ahmose

I've got a few minutes in between classes, so I thought I'd drop you a note. How are things back home? I'm missing everyone. It's good here but it's really hard work. We start very early in the morning, and the teachers are really strict. I'm still getting the hang of using the pens and inks, without getting smudges everywhere. It's not as easy as it looks!

WRITING HINTS AND TIPS

- If you're writing to a friend, you can use chatty, informal language.
- If you're writing to someone you don't know, use more formal language.
- Instead of a letter, you could write an email on the computer.
- Ancient Egyptian letters usually had two addresses — one at the top of the letter and the other on the outside of the papyrus so that it could be seen when the scroll was rolled up.

Pharaohs and wars

Ancient Egyptian society was headed by the pharaoh. Below him came the two viziers, the pharaoh's chief advisors. They oversaw the running of the country, and managed the pharaoh's household. Next came the nobles and priests, and, beneath them, scribes, soldiers and government officials. Below them came the craftsmen, and then the farmers, who made up the largest group. Slaves came at the bottom.

Great house

The pharaoh was the most powerful person in Egypt and was believed to be the god Horus, in human form. He was head of the government, commander-in-chief of the army, and high priest of every temple. The pharaoh was thought so holy that it was disrespectful to call him directly by name. Instead, he was given the title 'pharaoh', which means 'Great House'.

A statue of a pharaoh, wearing the ceremonial headdress.

A statue of a vizier, the pharaoh's chief adviser.

Royal dress

As a sign of his power, the pharaoh wore various crowns and headdresses. At times, he wore the double crown, which combined the white crown of Upper Egypt and the red crown of Lower Egypt. At other times, he wore a blue-and-white striped head cloth, with a gold image of a cobra at the front, which was believed to protect him from evil.

Did you know?

As part of the royal regalia, the pharaoh sometimes wore a false beard, made from goat's hair, to represent his god-like qualities. Early pharaohs also wore a bull's tail, hanging from the back of their kilts, as a sign of their bull-like strength.

A tomb painting of a pharaoh, sitting on his throne.

PHARAOH'S ADVICE

An ancient Egyptian poem, written by King Amenemhat I (ruled c. 1985–1955 BCE) to his son, Senusret I, gives him advice about ruling well.

Senusret, my son!
As my feet depart, my own heart draws near;
my eyes behold you ...
before the people who praise you.

You wear the white crown of a god.
The royal seal is in its place, assigned by me to you ...
Raise your monuments and establish your strongholds.
Fight for the wisdom of the wise.

Hatshepsut
(ruled c. 1478–1458 BCE)

The most remarkable female pharaoh was Hatshepsut. Her stepson, Thutmose III, became king at a very young age, and Hatshepsut was made regent. Later, she appointed herself pharaoh and ruled for about 20 years. One of her greatest achievements was to send a daring expedition to the land of Punt to bring back precious myrrh trees.

Did you know?

Very few women became pharaohs in ancient Egypt, and Hatshepsut was often called king, not queen. She wore the same royal regalia as a man, including the kilt, head cloth, cobra headdress and even the royal beard.

This statue of Hatshepsut shows her with a beard.

Thutmose III
(ruled c. 1479–1425 BCE)

The stepson of Hatshepsut, Thutmose III, was a great warrior. He fought many campaigns and, after Hatshepsut's death, created the largest empire Egypt has ever seen. For the first 20 or so years of his reign, he ruled jointly with Hatshepsut because he was too young to rule alone.

Akhenaten IV
(ruled c. 1353–1336 BCE)

Akhenaten gave up worshipping many different Egyptian gods, and decided to worship just one god – Aten, the sun god – instead. He built a new city, called Akhetaten, in Aten's honour. Akhenaten was married to Nefertiti who was known as the Great Royal Wife.

A stone carving depicting Akhenaten and Nefertiti.

Ramesses II
(ruled c. 1279–1213 BCE)

One of the greatest pharaohs, Ramesses II, is famous for his building works. He built a huge number of monuments, statues and temples, including two temples cut into the rock face at Abu Simbel. He also led the Egyptians against the Hittites, their greatest enemy.

A stone statue of Ramesses II at Abu Simbel in southern Egypt.

Write a cartouche

In ancient Egypt, the hieroglyphs for a pharaoh's name were written inside an oval shape. This was called a cartouche (see below). The oval represented a loop of rope, which was said to protect the name from evil spirits. Write your name in hieroglyphs and design your own cartouche.

Egyptians at war

The pharaoh was commander-in-chief of the Egyptian army and often led campaigns himself. Beneath him, there were several divisions of 5,000 men (foot-soldiers and charioteers). Each division was named after a god, such as Re, Amun and Ptah.

Foot-soldiers fought with spears, bows and arrows, axes and daggers, all made from wood and bronze. Chariots were pulled by two horses, with space for two soldiers to stand inside.

Battle of Kadesh

The Battle of Kadesh took place in 1274 BCE, between the Egyptians and the Hittites. Believing that the Hittite army was far away, Ramesses II approached the city of Kadesh, with only his bodyguard and one division. He was met by the full Hittite force, including thousands of chariots. Greatly outnumbered, Ramesses led his troops bravely until reinforcements arrived. Finally, the Hittites were forced to withdraw, although it is not clear if the Egyptians actually won, and their army suffered heavy losses.

Write a war report

Scribes accompanied the pharaoh into battle, and wrote up what happened each day. Imagine that you are a scribe at the Battle of Kadesh. Write a short report, which can be copied onto a temple wall. Remember to say what a great victory it was (even if it wasn't) and how brilliantly the pharaoh fought.

Writing History: Interview with a pharaoh

Imagine that you are a reporter from a local newspaper. You've been sent to interview Ramesses II. What questions would you ask him? Use the information in this chapter to help you come up with his answers. The first two questions have already been written.

WRITING HINTS AND TIPS

- Your interview should be made up of 10 questions.
- Ask some questions about Ramesses II's life and family, and about his feelings.
- Make sure that your questions are clear and easy to understand.
- Write the answers by imagining that you are very rich and powerful.

Daily Pyramid
The Pharaoh Interview

Q: Lord of the Two Lands, you have returned from Kadesh. How did the battle go?

A: It was brilliant – a triumph. I don't care what anyone says. The Hittites threw everything they could at us but we still managed to beat them back.

Q: What are your plans now that you're home?

A: I'm going to build a new temple. You can never have too many. I'll have the walls decorated with scenes from the battle, with me leading from the front, of course.

Gods and beliefs

The ancient Egyptians had hundreds of gods and goddesses. Some were worshipped throughout Egypt. Others were special to particular cities and towns. The gods were believed to have created the world, and to control all aspects of life. They helped and guided people, and had blessed the people by giving them the most beautiful land on Earth to live in.

Egyptian gods

Ra

Ra was the sun god who created the world. Each morning, legend said, he set sail across the sky in a boat, and the sun shone. At night, he sailed through the underworld, leaving the world in darkness. He is often shown with a falcon's head.

Osiris

Osiris was ruler of the dead, and god of the underworld (see pages 24–25). He was also believed to have brought grape vines and grain to Egypt. He is often shown with green skin, representing fertility, and is partially mummified.

Thoth

Thoth was one of the gods who stood on either side of Ra's boat. He was also god of wisdom and writing, and was the scribe to the gods. He is said to have invented hieroglyphs. He is often shown with the head of an ibis or a baboon.

Isis

Isis was one of the most popular goddesses in Egypt. She was the wife of Osiris, and was worshipped as the ideal wife, and mother to all the pharaohs. Her headdress represented an empty throne on which the pharaoh would sit.

Hathor

Hathor was the goddess of love, joy and beauty, and of motherhood. In tomb paintings, she is shown as welcoming the dead into the next life. She is usually shown wearing a cow's horns, with a setting sun between them.

Did you know?

Some animals, such as cats, bulls and ibises, were linked to the gods and goddesses, and were kept in their temples. When these sacred animals died, they were even mummified (see page 26). Millions of mummified animals have been found in Egyptian cemeteries.

The story of Osiris and Isis

Long ago, the sun god, Ra, made Osiris the first pharaoh of Egypt. Osiris ruled wisely and well with Isis as his queen. But jealous of his brother's success, Set plotted to kill him. He gave a great feast in Osiris' honour, where he brought out a beautiful wooden chest.

Set offered to give the chest to whoever fitted inside. Osiris was the first to try. The chest had secretly been made for Osiris, and it fitted him perfectly. Set slammed the lid down, and nailed it shut, then he threw the chest into the River Nile. The current carried it into the Mediterranean Sea. There, it was cast ashore and a great tree grew up around it.

After years of searching, Isis found the chest, and brought it back to Egypt. She hid the chest in the marshes, but Set saw it glittering in the moonlight. He pulled out Osiris' body, cut it into pieces, and threw it to the crocodiles. Slowly, Isis gathered the pieces, and put them back together so that Osiris could, at last, be buried with full funeral rites.

An artist's impression of Osiris about to try out the beautiful chest.

Write a spell for an amulet

The ancient Egyptians wore or carried charms, called amulets, to ward off evil spirits and illness. Some amulets were inscribed with magic spells that gave the amulet its power. Can you write a spell for an amulet, calling on the gods to protect you from harm?

A sacred scarab beetle amulet.

Egyptian worship

Every Egyptian temple was dedicated to a particular god or goddess, and their statue stood inside. It was believed that the spirit of the god or goddess communicated through the statue. Only priests and priestesses (see page 22) were allowed inside the temple. Ordinary Egyptians could go as far as the temple entrance to leave offerings and say prayers. If they wanted to ask the god a question, they paid a temple scribe to write it down and give it to one of the priests.

Massive statues of Ramesses guard the entrance to the Temple of Luxor.

Inside a temple

As the home of a god, a temple had to look impressive. It was built of stone, to make it last. The entrance was through a huge stone gateway, called a pylon. Outside stood tall obelisks, monuments to the sun god. The gateway led into one or more spacious courtyards. Beyond this was the hypostyle hall, where religious processions took place. Another hall led into the sanctuary, the most secret and sacred part of the temple. This is where the god's statue was kept, and only priests were allowed inside.

Carved columns inside the Great Hypostyle Hall in the Temple of Karnak.

Did you know?

The walls of Egyptian temples were decorated with scenes, carved into the stone and then brightly painted. Typically, they showed the pharaoh fighting in battles, and taking part in religious rituals with the gods and goddesses.

=◉= Being a priest =◉=

A temple wall carving showing an Egyptian priest.

Each temple had its own priests and priestesses, who took it in turns to go on duty. The rest of the time, they went back to their homes and families, and even did other jobs. A priest's main duty was to take care of the temple and look after the god's needs. Every day, the priest washed and shaved, then put on clean, white linen clothes and clean sandals. Then he entered the sanctuary to make offerings and say prayers. He then opened the shrine where the god's statue was kept. The statue was washed, dressed and given food, as if it were a living person. Afterwards, the shrine was closed and sealed.

The temple of Amun-Re at Karnak.

ORDER OF RITUALS

A papyrus scroll dating back to around 945 BCE sets out 66 rituals that priests at the temple of Amun-Re in Karnak performed every morning. At each stage, from entering the sanctuary to washing the statue, there were set words to recite. For example, as the priest opened the shrine doors, he said:

'The doors of heaven are opened. Hail to Geb, as the gods have said, established on their thrones. The doors of heaven are opened so that the gods of Osiris might shine.'

Writing History: Day in the life

Imagine that you are a priest in an Egyptian temple. It is your last day on duty, before you go home for a rest and to see your family. Write an account of the day. The first part has already been written. Using the information in this chapter, can you fill in the rest? You can talk about the temple you work in, how long you have been a priest, and how you felt when the pharaoh chose you for the job.

My day

Hi, my name is Herihor, and I'm one of the priests at the Temple of Amun-Re in Karnak. It was an honour to be chosen by the pharaoh, and this is a brilliant place to work. I can't tell you everything I do (it's top secret) but I can give you a glimpse of my day.

WRITING HINTS AND TIPS

- Start your account with a short introduction, giving your name and a few details.
- Write down events in chronological order (the order they happened).
- Describe your daily duties. Explain anything a reader might not know about.
- Include other details, such as information about your family and your early life.
- Remember to add your own thoughts and feelings to bring your account to life.

Death and the afterlife

The ancient Egyptians saw death as a step on the path to a better life in the Field of Reeds, a beautiful land somewhere to the far east. Before they could enter it, though, people had to prove that they had lived a good life on Earth. To do this, their souls had to make a difficult and dangerous journey through the underworld, and undertake various tests and ordeals.

Deadly journey

On the way to the Field of Reeds, souls had to pass through 12 gates, each guarded by a hideous monster, then cross a flaming lake of fire. Finally, they reached the Hall of Final Judgement, and their greatest trial. Standing before 42 judges, called the 42 Assessors, they had to swear that they were innocent of any wrong-doings during their lifetime.

Weighing the heart

If a person passed this test, an even greater ordeal lay in wait: the 'Weighing of the Heart'. Their heart was weighed against the feather of truth. If the person had led a wicked life, their heart would be heavier than the feather and they would be fed to a monster. If they had lived a good life, their heart would be lighter, and Osiris would welcome them into the Field of Reeds.

An illustration showing the Weighing of the Heart ceremony.

24

A copy of the Book of the Dead was placed in the coffin, between the mummy's hands.

BOOK OF THE DEAD

The *Book of the Dead* is a collection of spells, designed to guide souls through the trials they faced in the underworld. There are spells for finding the way, fighting off crocodiles, escaping from traps, and much more. There is even a spell (see right) for chanting at the Weighing of the Heart ceremony, to stop your heart giving you away!

O my heart of my mother!
O my heart of different forms!
Do not stand up as a witness against me,
do not be opposed to me in the trial,
do not be hostile to me in the presence
of the Keeper of the Balance.

Sometimes, a painted death mask was placed over the mummy's head, before the body was placed in its coffin.

Making mummies

For a dead person's soul to survive in the afterlife, the Egyptians believed that their body must be preserved. To stop bodies rotting away, they were mummified. First, embalmers washed the body. Next, they made a cut in the side, and removed the organs, apart from the heart. The body was then packed and stuffed with natron, a type of salt, to dry it out. After a few weeks, it was stuffed with sawdust, leaves and linen to make it look more lifelike. The body was then ready to be wrapped, using strips of fine linen. Between the layers, the embalmers placed amulets to protect the body on its journey through the afterlife.

Write an instruction manual

Write a mummification manual for an ancient Egyptian embalmer. Think about the order they have to do things in — make sure that you don't miss anything out. Then write clear, step-by-step instructions.

A tomb painting of a body being mummified.

Approximately 2.3 million blocks of stone were cut to create the huge Great Pyramid at Giza.

Pyramids and tombs

To make sure that their bodies lasted for ever, the pharaohs had massive tombs built. The most famous were the pyramids. It is thought that the shape of a pyramid represented the rays of the sun. Later pharaohs chose to be buried in tombs cut deep into rocky cliffs in the Valley of the Kings, on the edge of the desert, near Thebes. From the outside, the tombs looked quite plain, but inside, they were richly decorated with painted walls.

Did you know?

The Egyptians believed that the Field of Reeds was very much like Egypt, with homes and fields to look after. Wealthy people were buried with small figures, called shabti, in their tombs. In the next world, the shabti would come to life and do all the work for them.

Shabti figures found in an Egyptian tomb.

Tutankhamun's tomb

In November 1922, British archaeologist, Howard Carter, made an astonishing discovery. Buried deep beneath the ruins of tomb-workers' huts, he found a flight of steps, leading down to a sealed door. Behind a second door lay a room, filled with priceless objects, including chariots, life-sized statues and an exquisite golden throne. Carter had found the tomb of King Tutankhamun, who had died more than 3,000 years before.

Howard Carter discovering Tutankhamun's tomb.

A mummified pharaoh

The following February, Carter finally broke through into the burial chamber. At first, all he could see was a solid wall of gold. In fact, this was the first of four golden shrines, one inside the other. They contained a huge stone sarcophagus, with a nest of three coffins inside. The innermost coffin was made of solid gold. Inside it lay the greatest find of all – the mummified body of Tutankhamun, his face covered in a fabulous death mask.

Did you know?

Some people believed that the tomb was cursed, but was the rumour true? In the years following the discovery, several of Carter's team did indeed die in violent or unusual ways. One was poisoned; another died from an infected mosquito bite. But Carter himself lived until 1939, and died of natural causes, aged 64.

The extraordinary death mask of Tutankhamun.

Writing History: Newspaper report

Imagine that you are a newspaper reporter. You have been sent to Egypt to cover the sensational story of Tutankhamun's tomb. You arrive just as Howard Carter breaks through into the burial chamber and discovers the pharaoh's body. The opening of your report has been written for you. Don't forget to mention the pharaoh's curse …

THE ✿ DAILY ✿ DIG

18 February 1923

VALLEY OF THE KINGS, NEAR THEBES, EGYPT

TUT'S TOMB LATEST

LOST MUMMY FOUND

Three thousand years after his death, King Tutankhamun's body has finally been found, lying in a coffin of solid gold.

'I still can't believe it,' said Howard Carter, the archaeologist behind the find. 'I've dreamt of this moment for years and, at last, I've found my mummy!'

Covering the face is an exquisite golden death mask. Once this is removed and the mummy unwrapped, Carter will come face-to-face with the pharaoh himself.

WRITING HINTS AND TIPS

- Grab your reader's attention straightaway with a catchy headline.
- Start with the latest action, then work backwards to the discovery of the tomb.
- Use quotes from eyewitnesses to help bring the story to life.
- Use plenty of descriptive language to paint an exciting picture.
- Look at reports in newspapers and online to help you structure yours.

Glossary

amulet A small object that ancient Egyptian people carried, believing it gave them magical powers or protection.

archaeologist A person who studies the past, by looking at ancient places and objects.

chariot A two-wheeled vehicle, pulled by horses, used in racing and warfare.

civilisation The society, culture and way of life of a particular area.

cobra A highly venomous snake that spreads the skin of its neck into a hood when it is disturbed.

decipher Find the meaning of something that is difficult to read or understand.

dedicated Devoted to a task or purpose.

demotic A type of script used in ancient Egypt, which was easier to use that hieroglyphics.

embalmer A person who prepares a dead body for burial.

fertile Land that is rich enough to grow lots of crops.

Field of Reeds A form of paradise where ancient Egyptians believed their souls would live in an everlasting life.

funeral rites The ceremonies that are performed when a person dies and is buried.

ibis A large wading bird with a long neck, long legs and a curved bill.

inscribed When words or pictures are written or carved on an object.

inundation Another word for flood waters.

irrigation When water is brought from a river or lake to a farmer's fields.

kilt A knee-length, pleated skirt, worn by men in ancient Egypt.

linen A type of cloth woven from fibres from the flax plant.

mummified A body that has been preserved by having its organs removed and the rest treated with chemicals and wrapped in bandages.

myrrh A sweet-smelling gum produced by certain trees and used in perfumes, medicines and incense.

natron A type of salt found in dried lake beds.

ordeal A test, challenge or trial.

organ A part of the body, such as the heart, lungs and liver.

papyrus A reed used to make writing material, before paper was used. The reeds were cut into strips, pressed and dried to make a flat surface.

regalia Special clothing and jewellery, worn by members of royalty.

regent Someone who is given the job of ruling a country because the actual ruler is seen to be too young to rule.

ritual A special ceremony that is part of many religions or belief systems.

sanctuary The innermost and holiest part of an Egyptian temple.

soul The spirit of a human being or an animal that is thought to live for ever, even after death.

underworld Another word for the Next World, the kingdom of the dead, in ancient Egypt.

Further Information

Websites

www.britishmuseum.org/learning/schools_and_teachers/resources/cultures/ancient_egypt.aspx

Discover the culture and history of ancient Egypt with this British Museum website.

www.ancientegypt.co.uk/menu.html

Explore the British Museum's collection of objects from ancient Egypt.

www.bbc.com/bitesize/topics/zg87xnb/resources/1

Twelve class clips from the BBC about ancient Egyptian life.

www.pbs.org/wgbh/nova/ancient/explore-ancient-egypt.html

A website that allows you to take a tour inside the Great Pyramid and to walk around the royal burial chamber.

Books

The Best and Worst Jobs: Ancient Egypt by Clive Gifford (Wayland, 2015)
At Home with the Ancient Egyptians by Tim Cooke (Wayland, 2014)

Index

afterlife 18–19, 24–27
amulets 20, 26
archaeologists 5, 7, 28–29
army 12, 16

Battle of Kadesh 16–17
beliefs 18–24
Book of the Dead 25
burials 20, 24–29

Carter, Howard 28–29
cartouches 15
childhood 6
clothes 6–7, 12–15, 22

embalmers 26

family life 6
farming/farmers 4, 8–9, 12, 27
Field of Reeds 24, 27

gods/goddesses 6, 12–16, 18–24
  Amun-Re 16, 21–23
  Aten 15
  Hathor 19
  Horus 12
  Isis 19, 20
  Osiris 18–20, 22, 24
  Ra 18–20
  Re 16
  Set 20
  Thoth 19
government 10, 12
Great Pyramid, Giza 5, 27

hieroglyphs 10–11, 15, 19
Hittites 15, 16
homes 6–7, 27

irrigation 4, 8

jewellery 6–7

Karnak 22–23
kings (pharaohs)
  Akhenaten IV 15
  Amenemhat I 13
  Hatshepsut 14
  Menes 4–5
  Narmer 5
  Ramesses II 5, 15–17
  Senusret I 13
  Thutmose III 14
  Tutankhamun 5, 28–29

Lower Egypt 4–5, 12

masks, death 26, 28–29
mummies 19, 25–26, 28
mummification 18–20, 26

papyrus 7, 10–11, 22
pharaohs 9, 12–17, 20, 23, 27–29
priests/priestesses 6, 12, 21–23
pyramids 5, 27

religion 18–24
River Nile 4, 8–9, 20
Roman 5, 10

Rosetta Stone 5, 10

scribes 10–12, 16, 19, 21
shabti 27
shadufs 8
society 6, 12
soldiers 12, 16
statues 12, 15, 21–22, 28

temples 9, 10, 12, 15–17, 19, 21–23
tombs 7, 9, 10, 13, 19, 27–29
transport 4

underworld 18, 24–25
Upper Egypt 4–5, 12

viziers 12

wars 12, 15–17
weapons 16
weighing of the heart 24–25
writing 5, 10–11, 19

Peppa loves being kind.
Everyone loves being kind!

"Let's skip together with everyone,"
said Peppa.
"Yes!" cheered Suzy.
"What a lovely kind playgroup
we have!" said Madame Gazelle.

At playtime, Peppa and Suzy both
wanted to play with the skipping rope.
"It's my turn!" said Peppa.
"No, it's not," said Suzy. "It's *my* turn!"
"One . . . two . . . three . . . sorry,"
said Peppa and Suzy.

"What wonderful kind things, children!" said
Madame Gazelle. "Perhaps we should play
the One Kind Thing game every day!"
"Yes!" everyone cheered.

When they went back to playgroup, Peppa and her friends were excited to tell Madame Gazelle about their kind deeds.

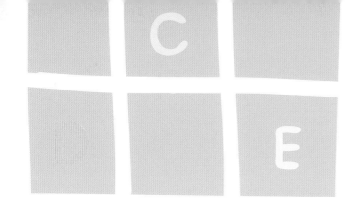

Mummy Dog made
Grandad Dog chuckle.

Mrs Zebra taught
Zaza and Zuzu Zebra
to make pottery.

Zaza and Zuzu gave their
pottery to Miss Rabbit!

Mummy Elephant
found Dr Elephant
his football boots.

Soon, everyone was doing one kind thing for someone else . . .

Danny gave his mummy a flower.

Zoe Zebra helped Mr Zebra post letters.

Mr Zebra gave Mrs Zebra a present.

Edmond found Emily Elephant's toy mouse.

Emily played the recorder for Mummy Elephant.

Granny Pig did one kind
thing for Grandpa Pig . . .

And Grandpa Pig did one
kind thing for Miss Rabbit.

So Mummy Pig did one kind
thing for Daddy Pig . . .

Daddy Pig did one kind
thing for Granny Pig . . .

"Can we help you with the shopping, Mummy?" asked Peppa.
"Yes, that would be very kind," said Mummy Pig, feeling happy.
"Then afterwards, will you please do one kind thing for someone else?" asked Peppa.
"Yes, of course," said Mummy Pig.

Peppa, George and their friends told their families
about the One Kind Thing game.
"What a lovely idea," Mummy Pig said to Peppa.

"Ooooh," said the children.
"The kind thing doesn't have to be big, just something that will make another person feel happy," explained Madame Gazelle.

"Now, children," said Madame Gazelle. "I have a little game for you. I call it my One Kind Thing game. To play, you have to do one kind thing for someone. Then, ask that person to do one kind thing for someone else."

"I like feeling happy," said Rebecca Rabbit.
"Me, too!" everyone cheered.

"Can I help George up?" asked Peppa.
"Of course, Peppa," said Madame Gazelle.
"That's very kind of you. When we are
kind, it makes others feel happy.
And it makes us feel happy, too!"

"If we know how others are feeling," said Madame Gazelle, "then we can help them."

After lunch, the children played hopscotch together.
George fell over and hurt his leg. He started to cry. "Waaah!"
"Poor George. I know how he feels," said Pedro Pony.
"I've hurt my leg before."

Bounce!

"What does everyone think Mandy
should do?" asked Madame Gazelle.
"Share!" cheered the children.
Mandy shared the ball with Danny.
They both felt happy.

Madame Gazelle asked Danny and Mandy
how they were feeling.
"I feel sad because I can't play," said Danny.
"I feel sad that Danny's sad," said Mandy.

Bounce!

Mandy was having lots of fun with the ball, and she
wanted to keep bouncing it all by herself.
"No," said Mandy. "You can play with it later instead!"
"That's not nice," said Candy Cat. "Danny looks sad."

Peppa and Suzy went out to the playground
to play with their skipping ropes.
Mandy Mouse was playing with a bouncy ball.
"Can I play bouncy ball with you, Mandy?"
asked Danny Dog.

"Very good," said Madame Gazelle. "If you have an argument with someone, stop and think about why you feel angry or upset. And think about how the other person is feeling, too."

". . . Sorry!" said Peppa and Suzy.
"I feel much better now," said Peppa.
"I don't feel angry any more."
"Me, too!" said Suzy. "I feel happy again."

"Wonderful suggestion, Edmond!" said Madame Gazelle. "Let's see what happens when they both say sorry at the same time. One . . . two . . . three . . ."

Madame Gazelle asked everyone what Peppa and Suzy should do.
"They should **both** be winners and say sorry for shouting," said Edmond Elephant.

"How are you feeling right now, Peppa?" asked Madame Gazelle.
"Angry!" said Peppa. "I won!"
"How are you feeling right now, Suzy?" asked Madame Gazelle.
"Angry!" said Suzy. "*I* won!"

At playtime, Peppa
and Suzy Sheep were
playing a game.
"I won!" shouted Peppa.
"No, *I* won!" shouted Suzy.

"And this one?" she asked, holding up a frowny face.
"Sad!" replied the children.
"Very good," said Madame Gazelle. "It's important we know what we are feeling and what others are feeling, too."

It was Well-Being Week at playgroup, and Madame Gazelle was talking about feelings with the children.

"What feeling does this picture show?" she asked, holding up a smiley face. "Happy or sad?"

"Happy!" called the children.

Peppa
is Kind

LADYBIRD BOOKS

UK | USA | Canada | Ireland | Australia | India | New Zealand | South Africa

Ladybird Books is part of the Penguin Random House group of companies
whose addresses can be found at global.penguinrandomhouse.com.

www.penguin.co.uk   www.puffin.co.uk   www.ladybird.co.uk

Penguin
Random House
UK

First published 2021
001

Licensed by

Printed in China

The authorized representative in the EEA is Penguin Random House Ireland,
Morrison Chambers, 32 Nassau Street, Dublin D02 YH68

A CIP catalogue record for this book is available from the British Library

ISBN: 978-0-241-47621-5

All correspondence to:
Ladybird Books, Penguin Random House Children's
One Embassy Gardens, 8 Viaduct Gardens, London SW11 7BW

MIX
Paper from
responsible sources
FSC® C018179

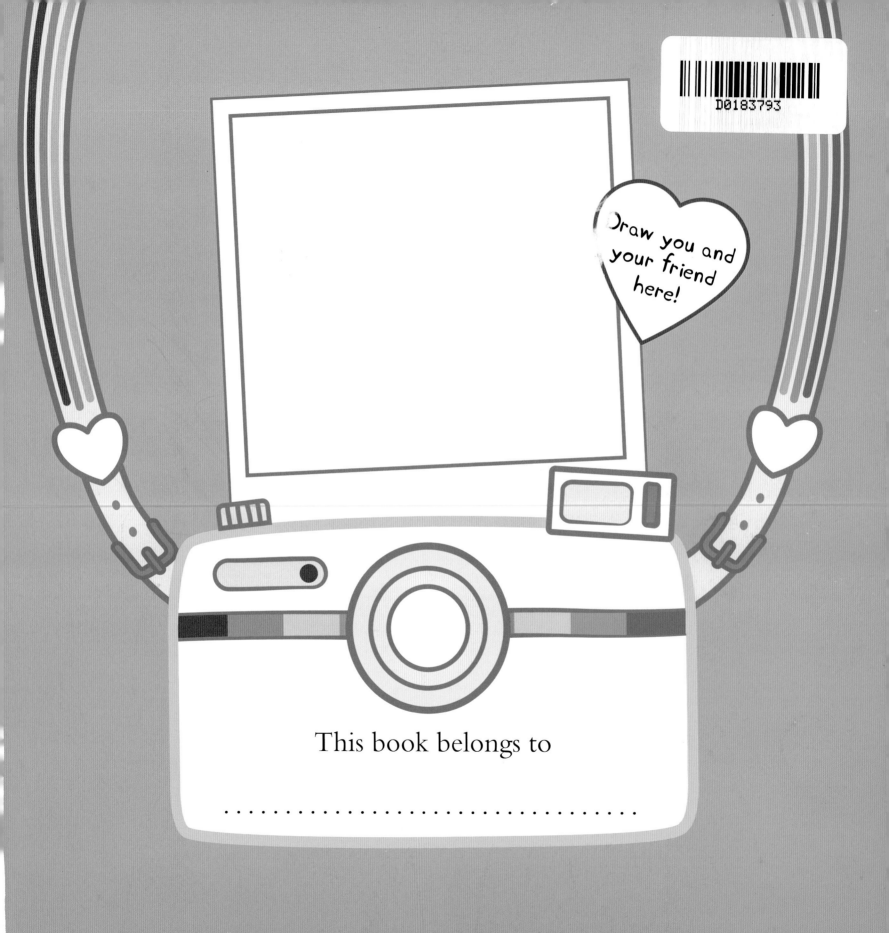

Draw you and your friend here!

This book belongs to

. . . .